THE 410 STRATEGY

HOW TO MAKE MORE MONEY

BY AARON G. ACOSTA

Table of Contents

Introduction

There are a number of self-help, business, and personal-development books available. I have red hundreds if not thousands of them. Many can help you improve some aspect of your life, work or self. Over the years I've found myself having the same conversation over and over with friends and others I've spoken to about life, business and making money. By repeating this process over and over I've been able to distill down three simple principles for how

to create success and make more money

doing something you enjoy. Stick with me to

the end and I'll share these insights and

more. My hope is that if you are stuck,

looking for a way to generate more income,

or are simply bored with your current work

situation, this will give you the tools you

need and the roadmap you need to get

where you want to go.

Chapter 1

Ask Better Questions

Have you ever wondered why some people seem to have success come easy while others appear to always be in a state of struggle and survival? Do you often imagine what your life would be like if you could just make as much money as others, or if you actually enjoyed what you did for a living? Do you wonder how some are able to transform their lives and go from fat to fit, from broke to wealthy, from shipwrecked to wildly successful? Is there some invisible force that decides which people become wildly successful, while others are chronically stuck living paycheck to paycheck while working a job they'd love to quit?

I have been on both sides of the equation. At one point my wife and I, along with our four boys (we now have 5) were homeless. We had to stay with friends for a brief couple of months while we got back on our feet. It's a pretty demoralizing feeling not being able to provide a place to sleep for your family and without the help of friends we would have certainly been forced to live out of our car.

Let me give you a little background on how my story started. I grew up with two older sisters and a younger brother. I don't remember being poor, I would have considered us a middle-class family. Now I think we struggled financially more than we would have liked to, but we made it work. My dad was a truck driver and my mom was in sales and management. From early elementary school age, I learned about hard work by going to work with my dad and also doing landscaping on the side to pay for things like my school clothes and school supplies. As a teenager, I was able to go to work with my mom and learned about sales and collections setting up payment arrangements with customers who had fallen behind on their jewelry store credit account. My parents worked a lot, they were always at work it seems. My father's work routine started early at 3:30 AM when he would get up and head to work. My mom's day was an early commute through traffic all the way downtown to open up the jewelry store she managed. A lot of times she worked late into the evening until the mall where the store was located was closed.

As a result of how I grew up, I wasn't afraid of hard work and because of that had a lot of independence. I moved out on my own at the age of 17 and was working while going to school. I've been a musician for most of my life and you've probably heard the joke, "what's the difference between a musician and a large pizza? (A large pizza can feed a family of four.) So yeah I worked a lot of odd jobs, not really anything you could call a career. I dropped out of high school in my senior year and got my G.E.D. I figured I could enroll in the local community college while playing more with the band I was a part of and still working a job. You see at the time, the only frame of reference I had for how to "succeed in life" was to work hard, get a job and make more money. I also saw a lot of other happy older people and their families and knew they made more money than my family. They drove nicer cars, lived in bigger homes in better neighborhoods. They enjoyed the activities I had only ever experienced in commercials on TV. I knew for them going to college wasn't an option it was assumed so I figured maybe if I could go to college I'd get a glimpse into their world and get even a small taste of "the good life." Keep in mind I don't know of anyone in my family that had gone to college and there certainly wasn't anyone pushing me to go. In that first semester, I registered for a full-time course load that included Comp I, College Algebra, and two other courses. I worked full time and had a 2-hour lunch break during the day. I'd rush over to the campus and get there just in time to catch my Comp I class and then rush back to work. I'd get off work at 5:30 and then rush back to campus and take my other courses. I was an A+ student in high school and I didn't even try. I'd soon learn college was a whole other ball game. The first day of college algebra left my head spinning. I couldn't take notes fast enough and it was like the guy was speaking a foreign language. On top of that his Asian accent made it extremely difficult to understand what he was saying. I was completely lost. After a week or two of seriously trying I knew I was in over my head. I decided to drop all my classes and try again the following semester. I did, however, keep my Comp I class going because I really enjoyed writing and my teacher was the best storyteller and just inspired me to be a better student. I remember him handing me my papers after grading them. He would always write on them "Really great paper!, A++ and then he would mark like a -40% on it and put my final score of what was usually an F, D or C. My grammar and spelling were horrible, but my writing was good! That's all the encouragement I needed to press on. I would try to be mindful of the mistakes I was making to improve my grades. I even had friends proofread my papers. I still hadn't learned any of the concepts I'm going to share with you in this book, but I still managed to scratch out a C- for the semester.

So after dropping out of high school, and plunging into my music career and college at the same time here is what I had to show for it. The band broke up, I still hadn't made my professional own album (a big goal of mine back then) and I had 3 credits in

Comp I. I was still working full time for $10 per hour at a small warehouse in Texas. Shortly after this, I met a girl, we fell in love, got married and started a family. So I never returned to college and here I was barely 22 years old and I had a son, a wife, bills, 3 college credits and about $360 per week to survive on after taxes.

I think back then the main questions I had playing on repeat in my head at the time were. 1.) How can I live on less? 2.) Who will give me a job making more money than I make now? You may not know this now, and I didn't know this then but, those are not good questions. It wasn't until much later in life that I would learn how important this is. The mind is a powerful supercomputer, in fact it is even more powerful than a supercomputer because when combined with your soul and your spirit it has the potential to create a virtually unstoppable force for creating change in your life and in the world around you. I hadn't yet learned the principle of asking better questions. They say that the definition of insanity is doing the same thing over and over but expecting different results. It didn't take long for me to begin to see the prison walls of insanity being built around me with each passing season. The worst part is I knew that I was the one building those very walls that would imprison me, but I didn't know how to stop it and I still didn't know how to go beyond that and become successful. The clock was ticking and I knew it, I knew I needed to find a way out of the rat race I had found myself in.

Chapter 2

Why We Don't End Up

Where We Hoped

Fast forward a few years and we now had two boys
and I had been working at a hospital in Dallas for
almost 5 years doing medical billing and appeals. I
started as a clerk and had been promoted twice to
Collector II and was actually doing the job of an
instructional designer, I just wasn't getting paid for

it, but that's a whole other story. While I enjoyed the instruction design portion of my job, prior to that most of my time was spent doing RNS reports. I think that stood for some kind of reconciliation status or something. Essentially every week we would get this massive stack of paper, an RNS report and we would have to go through it line by line, account by account and zero out what needed to be zeroed out and also appeal claims/accounts that were denied payment. You would work hard all week to get through that report and then on Monday morning another fresh mountain of papers would magically appear on your desk. At one point the monotony got to me and I took a tape measure to work. I measured out my little cubicle and discovered it was essentially a 4ft by 4ft cube. I then calculated how many hours I worked in that tiny cube every week for an entire year including the occasional Saturdays. I extrapolated that over my projected working lifetime to determine that eighty something percent of my life would be spent in that 4x4 cubicle. The majority of my life is defined by 16 square feet. It was enough to make me want to jump out a window. Something had to change but I didn't know what or how to change it. I had a wife and two boys depending on me to bring home the bacon and I wasn't even doing that very well. How could I selfishly want something more fulfilling for myself than my current 4x4 cubicle life? Why couldn't I just be thankful and just work hard at the work in front of me? Why did I always feel like there was more to life than just getting by, paying bills and living for the weekend?

Outside of work the passing of time only made it more evident that I was on the wrong path. I saw other couples buying homes, advancing in their careers, making more money, throwing better parties, putting their kids in private school, select clubs, going on real vacations and building their retirement accounts. It was a foreign world to me again. Here I was still feeling like a high school drop out except now I had a wife, kids, more bills and everyone else and life were passing me by. Living in a single wide mobile home in Euless Texas, two kids too young to understand how poor we were and still no college degree while working a job that inspired depression more than my greatness, was not where I had planned to be by my mid-twenties. The more self-aware I became the more I started to notice I was making some of the same decisions my parents had made financially that were not the best of choices. I remember talking with my wife one day while driving down 183 through the Mid Cities. I told her, "We are making bad choices financially that will keep us having to make more bad choices in the future." It was a small victory that I had recognized bad decision making, but I didn't exactly have the right recipe or full picture of how to be successful financially. I just knew that buying used cars off used car lots with high-interest loans was a dumb choice. My solution was to instead buy a brand new car off a new dealer car lot. I know some of you reading this are doing facepalm right now. My life was certainly a road of trial. The lessons I've learned have come from reflecting on my choices while living in the limitations and regret those choices resulted in.

The Rat Race

On one occasion a co-worker invited us over to his house for dinner and a game. The game was called "The Rat Race" and it was created by Robert Kiyosaki the author of Rich Dad Poor Dad. I remember feeling cool because here I was playing this game that other "success-minded" people played. It was all about making the best financial decisions and investments in order to get out of the rat race of trading time for money at some job and instead have your money making money for you. The goal in the game was to get your passive income from businesses or investments earn more monthly than your monthly expenses. For everyone in the room, it was just a good educational game. For me, it was a reminder that I was still just a rat in the race, going in circles every day without a clue as to how to get out. Sure the game taught you to make investments in stocks, business, assets, and real estate, but to do that you needed the money and here I was in my mid-twenties and I didn't know how to make money. I only knew how to make enough to barely cover my bills and trust me I didn't have a lot of bills. Most of the people playing the game with me had college degrees and careers. They were department heads, medical professionals and so on and I was just a broke kid, father, husband living paycheck to paycheck and only a flat tire or a layoff notice away from total financial ruin. At least now through work, I had friends who were more successful than me, but I still didn't know how to become successful and I wasn't sure I even wanted to do it the same way I had seen them do it. The idea of spending my life in a cubicle doing the office politics game didn't sound appealing to me at all. What's funny is at that age the window of opportunity for me was still wide open. Even with two kids and a wife, I could have chosen anything, music, business, real estate and I could have been successful but, that's a lesson we will discuss later.

The main point is I wasn't where I wanted to be in life. Whatever recipe I was following for success it wasn't working. In fact, it was moving me in the opposite direction that I wanted to go. What I needed was to find the exit ramp off the freeway to failure. I needed to ask better questions and find a better recipe. The problem is my thinking was broken. If your thinking and perspective are bad, the questions you ask will be the wrong questions and as a result, you'll get bad solutions to the wrong problems that will send you sprinting off in the wrong direction chasing the wrong things for the wrong reasons. It's a domino effect with the power of compounding interest over time. So in the next chapter lets take a better look at why we don't end up where we want to be and let's start putting into place the proper framework for achieving personal success.

Overwhelmed & Uninspired

Several years had passed since I was working in Dallas at that hospital. I had moved from Texas to Oregon, to Florida, to Colorado, to Michigan back to

Texas and now back to Oregon. I left with my family in 2006 to move to Oregon to pursue my dream. I have been a musician and a worship leader since I was barely a teenager. This is not a book about spirituality but I will weave in some lessons I've learned along those lines because it's hard to separate business and purpose from spirituality, in fact, I think it's a tremendous mistake to attempt to do so. Prior to leaving Texas, I would not have defined myself as successful. In my mind, I did equate living your passion or "doing what you're called to do", with being successful. At the time I told myself if I can just work full-time as a worship leader then I'll be on the path to success because to do what you were born to do is the greatest definition of success, or so I thought. The problem is that "what you are called to do," is easily influenced by the questions we ask ourselves, our perspective based on our experiences, our surroundings, and those people closest to us. If we have not learned how to truly think outside of our experiential and environmental limitations then our thinking is in fact extremely small, limited and often misguided.

From about 2006 to 2012 I saw a lot of the US, made a lot of great memories and made new friends. I learned a lot more about myself and discovered some new passions and influences. I had lived my dream of working as a full-time worship leader, made more money than at any other time previously. My wife and I now had 4 boys and in spite of our small successes we were still paycheck to paycheck and although I had already been laying the foundations for a major shift in the direction of our life, most if not all of that time could be defined as one major financial struggle or set back after another. During that time I had gone back to school through Liberty University online and was almost done completing my Bachelors in Religion with a minor in business. This was a personal goal for me as I always regretted not graduating with my class my senior year, although I wouldn't have wanted to miss the time I had spent playing guitar for a band that I was with during that time. I have a ton of great memories from those adventures. Now I had an education, I had pursued my dream, had worked in the field I was most passionate about and yet here I was around thirty-three years old and I was basically homeless with four kids and a wife. A string of bad luck had dissolved my small savings account and we wound up in Oregon with no home, no job and a used Plymouth Voyager with I think over 240,000 miles on it. Some friends from a church we served at previously in Oregon graciously let us stay in one of their rooms while I hunted and secured a job. We were going into the holiday season and I remember sharing a single bed (not a queen, not a full, but a single) with my wife while our three older boys slept on the floor like little enchiladas rolled up in their blankets. Our baby boy Judah had his crib set up in the closet and we all crammed into this tiny room. Thankful to have a roof over our head and scared to death of what tomorrow held.

Around two years prior to that moment, I had only ever read books about spirituality. I was really passionate about studying the bible and any book related to studying scripture. It was during our time in Detroit though when one of the pastors there taught me how to sell used center caps on eBay. I needed a way to provide for my family and still allow us time for the ministry we were involved in. I quickly absorbed what he taught me and pretty soon I was making more money working for myself than I had made at any regular job I had had and I was only working one or two hours a few days of the week. I had won the lottery! There is nothing materially more valuable than having the freedom to determine what you do each day with your time while still being able to provide for yourself. I think that is what they call financial freedom. It sure felt like freedom to me. For the first time, I could take care of my family and I wasn't stuck in some 4x4 cubicle. We weren't getting rich and we didn't have a lot of expenses at the time anyway but definitely shifted my thinking. I had two thoughts during that first week when I started making a lot of money online. First, I thought I will never work for someone

else doing something I don't like again and second,
I am going to consume everything I can get my
hands on about online business and online
marketing. My focus shifted from only reading
books on spirituality to absolutely devouring
anything and everything I could find on business
and marketing. If I was in the car I had a podcast
going, if I was laying in bed I was reading an ebook,
on the train on the pot, waiting for a table at a
restaurant. It was all-consuming and insatiable. It
wasn't a degree in business which I have to say
had done little to nothing to help me in my quest for
better income and work opportunity. My book,
podcast and kindle collection were a master's
degree in business and marketing taught not by

professors, but practitioners. Guys and gals that were in the field every day using the tools and processes of an emerging world and way of life. The digital nomads as they would call them.

It was through the books and podcasts that my perspective on what was possible began to change. The entrepreneurs in those books and audio files and youtube videos became my mentors and business coaches. They became the voice in my life that I never had. They introduced me to one of my great passions, online marketing. See I had two years of this knowledge just building up inside of me, new perspectives, new ways of thinking, better questions being asked. I learned about eCommerce platforms, digital advertising, psychology, persuasion, leverage, automation and so much more.

The most important evolution came in my thinking. That's where everything begins or dies. I had not yet taken any massive action on what I was learning other than keeping my online hub-cap store going. We drove all over the US pulling a little 5x8 trailer behind me that had my hubcaps in boxes in them. Since I could ship them from anywhere I could run my business from anywhere. This is part of how we wound up in Oregon with no job, no house and almost no money.

During our two or three week stay with those friends from our church, I landed a position with a local life insurance agency selling life insurance. Those were tough times. I would drive from one appointment to the next 7 days a week sun up to sun down listening to audiobooks and podcasts in my van. During the day I was being inspired by people like Les Brown, Zig Ziggler, Jim Rohn, Pat Flynn, Tony Robbins, John Lee Dumas, Brendon Burchard, Molly Pitman and Greg Hickman just to name a few. At night I was tired emotionally, physically and spiritually. I remember driving home from appointments in Salem, taking the long freeway drive north back to Hillsboro at night. I'd have the podcast or audiobooks playing but the only thing I heard were the two voices in my head.

One voice was telling me to keep learning, don't

give up, give it your all, tomorrow your

breakthrough is coming. That voice was easily

drowned out and overpowered by the other voice

telling me to drive my vehicle into one of the pillars

holding up the overpass. It told me if I killed myself

then my wife would meet a better man who could

provide better. My kids would have a more able

father and their futures would be bigger and

brighter if I was out of the picture. All I wanted was

the best for them and I felt that my twelve or so

years as a father, husband, and provider had

proven that I was not good at being that for them.

That voice told me they would be better off without

me in the picture. I would just stare out as far as the headlights would let me and kept driving.

Eventually, I did learn a valuable lesson. A lot of people that are successful simply work way harder than everyone else. Don't get me wrong I was a hard worker. Show up early, leave late. Never stop learning, ask for more work, do more than is expected, etc. But there is another level of "hard work." There is the "whatever it takes to win" level of work. It is not defined or limited by office hours, job descriptions and such. It does not entertain excuses or even talk about why something won't work. It only focuses on, it must work, I must win, whatever it takes, failure is not an option. It is like

Yoda says, "Do or do not, there is no try."

After our short stint with our elderly friends from church, we ended up moving in with our best friends from the same church. That was completely humbling and embarrassing but they were lifesavers for us. We spent Christmas living in their second living room. Every time their friends or family came over I wanted to crawl under a rock and die. Here I am 33 years old with four boys and a wife and I'm living in my best friend's living room. This is most definitely not where I had planned to be by this time in life. They were so gracious and loving and never judged us or tried to give us tough love. I wish I could say I'm as gracious when I was on the other side of the equation in similar situations but I'm not. I'm a prideful ass who is still in process but thank God for good friends.

So this new superpower I discovered, the "whatever it takes" type of hustle. I began to apply that to my job. Now I can see why some people kill themselves, burn out and join the funny farm. Because long term that type of drive is simply not sustainable and it's not healthy. In a short time, I went from living with friends to securing our own apartment and I even bought myself a Mercedes Benz to drive to all my work appointments. It was more money than I needed. Shortly after moving into the apartment my wife and I also launched an online business. I married the knowledge I had been amassing the last two years with skill and knowledge she had been amassing for over a decade and boom, we were in business. The first time we launched a business things were very different. My wife and I decided we wanted her to be home with the kids rather than putting them in daycare. So when the doctor she worked for retired and her position evaporated we decided to launch her photography business. I'd like to tell you it was a Cinderella story and that it went amazing but that was not the case. Both our cars were repossessed and our house was foreclosed on. Our credit was destroyed and we were extremely tight financially but, we stuck to our guns and my wife stayed home and raised our boys and I wouldn't change a thing. She was the best thing for them and I have amazing sons now as a result of her love and care with them. That and although her business didn't skyrocket it hummed along year after year providing a little spending money every now and then. It was in Oregon that we moved into those apartments and a switch was flipped in both of us. You see for me, I had great success selling insurance and even was invited to their Top Gun training event where I would be trained and compete alongside the best new insurance agents in the nation. I went to California and competed and won the Top Gun award! It was also during that time that I had an important mental shift. A total game changer that I think everyone needs to have. I went from having

limiting beliefs and having that inner voice telling

me my family would be better off without me, to

truly believing I could do anything. I could create

any future I wanted, it was really possible. It wasn't

a hope, it wasn't positivity, it was absolute F#$^Y#R

certainty! At the same time, my wife was like a

momma bear protecting her cubs. Being homeless

was the spark that lit an entrepreneurial fire in her

too.

You see some people never change. They go

through life complaining about their job, their boss,

their lack of income, their lack of opportunity etc.

And they never ever change. It's always someone

else's fault, the economy, their boss, their parents, etc etc. Then there are those people who become inspired by something, they become inspired towards change. They see something, a song, a movie, a conversation with a mentor, a positive experience creates a shift in their thinking that makes them believe they are capable of so much more. Something inspires them into creating the change they need in their life.

Then there are some people who discover they are capable of so much more because they have no choice. It's do or die. Their employer goes belly up, their spouse dies, their safety net evaporates, they are forced out of their comfort zone and they do whatever it takes to survive and in the process end up creating massive change in their life and massive success that they didn't know was possible until it became absolutely necessary.

It reminds me of a podcast I listened to from a real estate investor back in the day. This is an awesome story. I'll tell you all about it in the next chapter!

Think about these questions before you move on. Are you the type of person who has been inspired to maximize your potential and time on this planet? Or are you the person who got backed into a corner and discovered you were capable of so much more because there was no other option? Or are you the person who is in the struggle and is neither inspired or forced into action, but rather has passively accepted their fate and is letting life push and shove them in whatever direction the winds of circumstance are blowing? Hopefully, you are open to becoming the first. If you are ready to discover that you are capable of so much more, and if you are ready to be given the tools to unlock that then continue reading. In the next chapter, we are going to start doing some exercises together as I unpack what I've learned and refined over the years and teach you how to create more success in your life.

Chapter 3

Breaking Out Of The Impossible Box

Next I want you to go through a series of exercises.

Don't just read the book and fly through to the next

section but take time to do each exercise and really

spend time thinking through them. Find a quiet

place to do this where you won't be distracted or

rushed and really work to put yourself into the scenarios mentally and emotionally. If you struggle with limiting beliefs, those beliefs have to be identified and deconstructed so that you can think outside of the limitations that are holding you back. Ask any successful person and they can point towards disciplines and actions they have taken to achieve that success, but they would also point towards a shift in thinking that started it all.

100 Ways To Make A Buck

I want you to imagine that you wake up the next morning and the business you work for has shut down and you are out of a job. In fact, imagine that the entire industry or type of work is no longer available. I want you to also imagine that no company is hiring anywhere. Not a single job is available that you can apply for. Think about what this means for you and your family and those that depend on you. Now take out a sheet of paper and write down all the ways you could make a buck without someone hiring or giving you a job. Try to come up with enough ideas to fill the sheet of paper front and back. This is an exercise to help you expand your thinking and recognize opportunities that you might have overlooked. It also helps you to get out of a thinking rut. As we age we are prone to conform to routines and are able to only see in our minds the places we've already been and the solutions we usually gravitate to. This can force you to think outside of those well worn mental paths and safe places.

Creating A New Frame of Reference

Now I want you to imagine that you and I are sitting at your favorite pub or coffee shop. We are having a drink and talking about life. It's in the evening and you're tired from a long day of work. Now imagine that I ask you this question. "Hey, how certain are you that you will earn a million dollars next year from your real estate investments?" Ok, so what was your immediate reaction? Did you bawk at the idea of even making any money in real estate? Did you reply "absolutely certain?" If you are like most of the people I've asked this, they would say "You're crazy, I'm not going to make any money in real estate next year, let alone two million dollars. I would then ask, "Yeah but could you?", and they would respond, "most definitely not." To which I would reply, "Why not?"

And as sure as the sunrise I would get a few answers. 1.) Because I've never done it. 2.) Because I don't know how 3.) Because it's impossible 4.) I don't know how and I wouldn't even know where to start. Next I would say, "Okay, now let's reset and clear your mind. Then I would begin again. I want you to imagine that your great, great, great, great grandfather was a real estate tycoon. Like Rockefeller type of success. He was a multi-millionaire in real estate, and so were all his kids and grandkids. In fact your family tree is flooded with multi millionaires, and they all made their fortunes in real estate. Your mom and dad and brothers and sisters are all millionaires from real estate. Everyone in your family makes real estate look so easy. Now let me ask you again, "Can you make a million dollars in real estate?" Now you probably responded a few different ways. 1.) Probably 2.) Definitely 3.) It would be impossible not to. Then I'd ask you why and you'd say something like…"because everyone in my family has done it, then I can do it too", or, "I'll just ask them to show me how.

There are so many things going on in this conversation right now that it's impossible to fit it all into this book and there is also a lot missing from not being able to interact with you personally and hear your tone and see your facial expressions but unless you are severely broken in your thinking and self confidence, then your responses would be similar to the conversation we imagined above. So I want you to notice how the first time I asked if you could make a couple million dollars in real estate next year you said no. You said it would be impossible because you've never done that before. Then by simply changing a few EXTERNAL scenarios, you suddenly believed it was at least possible, if not highly likely. The first thing to recognize is that so much of our life, our circumstances, options, opportunities, abilities are all seen and influenced by our experiences and our surroundings. If you do not realize this, then your thinking may be extremely limited. That's not an insult. The mind is a muscle, it just means your potential for explosive growth and change is massive. If your momma used to tell you, you can be anything you want to be, well, it's kinda like that. Until you can honestly say that life is one massive buffet of experiences and opportunities and you can put whatever you want on the plate, then your thinking is limited. Yes there is a little thing called your "window of opportunity" but we'll discuss that in a later chapter. For now it's important to realize that your thinking is limited and that you need to throw off those limitations. Another important thing to recognize from this exercise is just how much our circle of influence and experiences plays into what we believe is possible for us. As soon as you were told everyone in your family had built fortunes in real estate you would feel stupid if you couldn't do it to. Hence your belief that you could was suddenly boosted. The people we surround ourselves with, the books we read, the shows we watch, the podcast we listen to, the friends we associate all play a major role in determining what our expectations are from life and from ourselves. By simply making concrete adjustments in what we feed our mind and what and who we surround ourselves with, we can shift the trajectory of our thinking and our success. Another interesting thing to pull from this exercise is emphasized by some of your responses. If you said you probably could make a couple million dollars in real estate because you could ask one of your relatives how to get started and achieve that level of success then you illustrated two important points. First, the importance of a mentor. Someone who has already done what you want to do. Secondly, the importance of the RECIPE. If there is something you want to do, achieve or become that feels or appears to be impossible, realize that someone somewhere.. Actually thousands of people before you have likely done that very thing. You want to make an amazing lasagna? There are endless recipes for the lasagna, both that will actually make a great lasagna, but also a lasagna tailored to your specific likes and preferences. Want to make a million dollars? There are thousands of people, examples, RECIPES that can get you there. Some are good, some are better but there are plenty. You just need to find the right recipe. Even better if you can learn that recipe from a mentor that can walk you through the process.

A Terminal Illness Scenario

Now I want you to take a break from reading. Get a cup of coffee, clear your head and then come back to this exercise after 20 or 30 minutes. Now for this exercise I want you to imagine that we are sitting together and talking at your favorite coffee shop. When you picture this in your mind make sure your mental image is vivid. What is the weather like outside? Is there sunlight pouring in through the windows, what is the temperature? What are you drinking and how does it taste? Are you there? Ok let's begin.

I want to tell you about a story I heard on a podcast from a real estate investor. This was almost a decade ago so I can't remember the investor or his podcast but the story stuck with me. There was this married woman that had three kids and lived in an average middle class home. They were comfortable with their average home and their salaries of around $40K per year. Things were going well and they were content. She and her husband were both teachers when unexpectedly, in the same week, both she and her husband lost their jobs. Her and her husband quickly found themselves in a tough place. Bills stacking up and no income. Her husband decided to bail on her and the kids and disappeared. At the same time one of her sons became very sick. The doctors told her they only expected him to live another six weeks. So almost overnight her world was turned upside down. Her job was gone, her bills were stacking up, and her husband had left, all while she had to watch her son's health slip away with no hope from doctors that he would survive.

Can you imagine the physical and emotional stress this woman and her kids had endured in such a short period of time. For most people that would be enough to bury us for good. What takes place next is simply awe inspiring.

So her son ended up surviving beyond the six weeks and actually started to recover. They eventually discharged him home but not without the need for a lot of home medical equipment. He was still in a hospital type bed and depended on several machines to help him breathe and slowly recover.

Only days after being discharged from the hospital she was at home caring for her son when there was a knock at the door. She opened the door and a man from the electric company handed her a bright red paper. You can imagine what this was. It was a notice that if her account wasn't brought current her electricity would be shut off. She shut the door and was lost in a daze as her eyes drifted back and forth between that bright red notice in her hand and her son lying there in bed connected to all that medical equipment. She knew if they disconnected her electricity he could die without the machines that were helping him breathe and recover.

In that moment she could have crumbled under the weight of everything going on in her life. Instead she grabbed a sheet of paper and started frantically writing down everything she could do to make money fast. She didn't leave out anything. Her page was filled with everything from selling my possessions to selling drugs. She knew she needed a plan, she knew failure wasn't an option, she had to find a way to make a lot of money fast, her son's life depended on it! During her writing she recalled that a friend of hers was a real estate investor and had at one time offered to teach her how to get started. She contacted him and he agreed to show her how to make a living as a real estate investor. She describes the next six months as just a frantic zombie-like blur. She had gone into momma bear mode. The next six months flew by and during it she was able to get those electric bills paid and see her son recover. What's inspiring is that not only did she manage not to crumble under the weight of her circumstances, she actually achieved what most would think is impossible. In a mere six months she had amassed an investment portfolio worth 3.2 million dollars. This six months of all out focused effort would generate her an annual cash flow of over $900,000. Impossible you say? It gets even better. Her boys grew up seeing what their mom was capable of and were able to learn from her. You could say they had a great recipe and an excellent mentor. At the time when I heard the podcast her once sick son had become a millionaire

at age fourteen and was now a public speaker

traveling the world delivering speeches on how we

are all capable of so much more than we attempt.

Her other youngest son had racked up his first

million by age eleven also in real estate.

This story perfectly demonstrates something I've

learned over the years of studying people,

personal-development and reading countless

numbers of books and biographies. Typically

people fall into three categories. Either they see or

experience something positive that makes them

think differently. They become inspired toward

greatness, or, they experience something terribly

negative and that motivates them to create massive change. In the first scenario their thinking is conditioned to believe they can do or achieve something great. This can happen in an instance or overtime as the result of the environment they are surrounded by. In the second scenario it's not about a person believing they can do, achieve or become, but more so that they must, like a do-or-die scenario. The problem is that many people experience neither. They go through their entire life existing somewhere in between those two extremes living "comfortably miserable" and as a result never realize just how much more they are capable of becoming. They are neither inspired toward greatness, nor forced by circumstance to become more than they are presently manifesting. The result is a small life of wasted potential unfulfilled dreams, mediocrity and regret.

For me I sort of experienced both ends of the spectrum until a shift was finally created for me. Everything begins in your thinking. On one end I was fueling my mind with books, audiobooks, podcasts of these great entrepreneurs who were creating businesses and solving problems while amassing wealth. They were living life on their terms. I studied them and their skill sets voraciously. I was reprogramming my mind with positive aspirations of what I could also accomplish once I had acquired those same skill sets. I thought, if I can learn what they know and do what they do, I can have what they have and live like those guys. At the same time I was in such great need financially that I absolutely had to win. I would either achieve success or wind up on the street and possibly lose my family. All at the same time I was acquiring the skills, while being inspired to create a vision of the life I wanted and being motivated by the reality that not achieving my dream was simply not an option because the cost of failure to do so was just too great a loss. All of these things added up till eventually I reached a moment of clarity. My switch was flipped. I suddenly realized I could become and do anything I wanted. So now finally, everything came into alignment with that awareness and conviction. It's like moving from "I hope…" to "I'm certain" or, "I wish…" to, "I'm absolutely certain I will…". This may seem like something small but trust me, it's massive. When you finally get out of your own way, anything is possible. Most people have self sabotaging beliefs and mental programming that is running all the time at the subconscious level. You do the same things and never even enter the realm of asking yourself the right questions. You live this life that just doesn't feel quite right, like the real you is just dormant on the inside and you know it's there but you don't even know how to have a conversation with that person, or what you would talk about. That's okay.

This book is also for you. We'll dive into how to get started in the next chapter.

Chapter 4

Getting Clear

Do you wake up in the morning to the sound of an alarm clock ringing in your ear? Dragging yourself through your morning routine like there are concrete blocks molded around your feet. The thought of venturing off to work is so uninspiring you have to drink a 5 gallon bucket of coffee just to amp yourself up enough to get out the door. You come home exhausted and unmotivated only to repeat this process again and again, until you reach the weekend where you get to be a free person again? The captain of your own destiny, at least for a day or two. You repeat this cycle every month and hopefully manage to earn enough to pay some bills and just barely get by. You secretly hope something will change and at the same time feel so stuck you're suffocating.

If this describes you, then think about this. Most people I've spoken to that are stuck in this cycle say the same thing. If I just made a little more money, or if I could just get a little more of this or a little less of that, then I'd be good. The problem is that a little more or a little less isn't really that much of a change from the situation you are already in. I call it living the uninspired life.

What if you could capture or create a vision for your life that was so inspiring it would keep you up late and make your spring out of bed early each day. Imagine if this vision did more than just get you buy with a little cushion, what if it met all your needs and allowed you to invest in your biggest dreams? What if this great new vision for your life had you contributing at the highest level, employing all of your unique God-given talents and passion? I've had so many conversations with friends and even other professionals that are desperately wanting something different that they simply can't seem to define. What they are essentially saying is they want an escape, something, anything different than their present reality. Marketing companies and industries have made billions off the idea of "escaping reality." Whether that's through stimulants, depressants, weekend getaways, lifestyle changes and on, they have tapped into people's desperation and desire for change. So you've been fooled or sold on the idea of escaping, doing less, or nothing at all. There is nothing wrong with downtime and taking a break, but you may have heard that saying, "Rather than seeking a vacation, how about designing a life that you don't need to take a vacation from." Maybe that's why so few people ever truly exit the rat race. Just like a ship sitting in the water with no sail up, no course charted, and no rutters turning, a life seeking to simply escape to nothing and for no good reason won't exactly journey anywhere. It won't generate enough force to allow it to break free from the current. The masses are caught in the current of "the way things are", and are simply seeking to do nothing or escape because they don't have a compelling vision to "escape" to. That's not your fault, so many of us lack a mentor and have been sold on the same ideals for how to create a successful life. We've been sold by marketing, our employers, by observing what everyone else does, and even by our government and educational systems. We are too busy, too distracted, and too mentally fried to even begin thinking in a way that leads us to real success.

What does real success look like? To me true success is when you are living your highest values and convictions. When what you truly believe is in alignment with what you say and do. When all of those things are tied to actual values and core convictions. When you design a life for yourself with a clear vision, and purpose that is in alignment with your core convictions, then you are free to contribute at the highest level.

My desire here is not to rewrite the countless books and teachings that have been written on these types of subjects. It's also not to curate some stale, stagnate formula for how to think. It's simply to have the conversation with you that I've had with myself and so many others. Unfortunately we are not sitting across from each other, exchanging ideas back and forth. Normally in these conversations your response tells me all I need to know in order to continue peeling away the layers of unbelief, bad programming and limited thinking, and trust me there are many, many layers. See the problem is every exchange is like a step forward and with each step forward your mind and emotions are going to put forward challenges, rebuttals and downright roadblocks to ideas I'm asking you to wrestle with. See you may be trapped inside the box of limited thinking, limited or experiential sight, and the limited scope of your immediate surroundings. So you will only benefit from these ideas or "conversations", to the degree that you are willing to challenge yourself each time you present a roadblock, excuse or anecdotal evidence for why things are the way they are. This is amplified since I'm not with you to hear your rebuttal or reply and challenge it for you. I should also warn you of the simple common trap most get stuck in.

Chasing the smaller goals of survival, escape and shallow or surface level needs will not bring you to a compelling vision and purpose for your life. Like goal setting they can help you achieve more than you have in the past. They can help you change your circumstances but they won't help you contribute at your highest and maximize your potential. What you need to do is get clear and specific about what you want and more importantly why. This may seem harsh or judgy but the "WHY" you come up with is directly related to your "CORE VALUES." The quality of your CHARACTER will determine your CORE VALUES and the quality of your CORE VALUES will determine the quality of your WHY which will dictate the quality and effectiveness of your clarity and vision you end up designing for yourself. Poor character results in weak or poorly defined values which translates into small, selfish and self-centered goals which fail to create a fulfilling life and compelling vision to get us there. The stronger and better your core values and convictions are the easier it will be to attain clarity and discernment when it comes to making tough decisions and sacrifices. My father always told me, "The good things in life are the enemy of the best." My hope for you is that by holding strong core values and character, you can move from bad, beyond good and into the best life possible.

So let's begin. One simple question with endless possible answers. You'll have to revisit this question again and again as you seek to understand yourself and as you grow in knowledge, experience, wisdom, and understanding. My question for you is, what do you want?

WHAT DO YOU WANT?

It's a very simple question that most people only ask themselves at a surface level. What do you want? What do you want that you are not willing to compromise on? What do you want that if you don't get will result in massive regret? This shouldn't be confused with things like...

What do your parents want?

What does society tell you that you should want?

What do you think you need?

What does everyone else want?

What do you think is possible?

What do you think you're worthy of?

What do you think you've earned?

What do you think you deserve?

What do you think you are owed?

What are you willing to settle for?

What do you want? Take some time and write out exactly what you want and when you do be specific and descriptive. Think through and write out your why, Make sure the why is tied to or has one of your core values as it's foundation and that it is important to you and also to others beyond yourself. Disclaimer: some people only think of themselves and some people only think of others and neglect themselves. You need to have a balance when doing this exercise. Kind of like when the oxygen mask drops in an airplane. They always tell you to put your mask on first before attempting to help others. In this instance make sure you aren't killing the golden goose. Getting clear about what you want should be designed in a way that you are always increasing and expanding your potential so that your highest contribution is always increasing and expanding. You'll severely limit your potential if your vision doesn't have a healthy amount of balance to it.

Chapter 5

The Shawshank Redemption

There are three things that greatly impact your ability to create change in your situation or circumstances. Three things that can help you in creating the massive change or shift you want to see in your life. In the 1994 film the Shawshank Redemption Andy Dufresne, played by actor (Tim Robbins), is a successful banker that is convicted of murdering his wife and is sentenced to two life sentences in prison. Although he is truly innocent he finds himself subjected to the cruel realities of life in prison during the 1940's. During the film you may find yourself rooting for Andy because you know he's innocent and he's a good guy, but despite all that he still finds himself imprisoned for life. We can relate to that on some level because sometimes despite feeling like we do everything we are supposed to do, we still end up imprisoned by life, bills and limitations of our time, energy and resources. It's an excellent story and I recommend you see the movie, but more than that, to me the movie illustrates the main points I want to get across in this book. As I look back and examine in my life what caused things to shift and change for me I see those same principles modeled out in the movie. Some people innately know these, others are taught or modeled them by people that are influential in their life. For me I was never taught these things and I wasn't surrounded by people who modeled them for me personally. My goal is to give those who are frustrated and trapped in a cycle of limited opportunity, a true roadmap to their own definition of success, an escape from the limitations of the prison they may find themselves in. For you it may be a job, a vicious cycle of unhealthy relationships, or a search for your purpose or passion. Like Andy Dufranse, you may find yourself stuck in a prison of your own, we won't argue in this chapter about whether that's any fault of your own, I want to simply focus on identifying the three things that can help you escape and earn your freedom back. I say earn because you do have to do the work, your patterns and habits will have to change, but change is possible and so is freedom.

If you've seen the movie then you know that Andy Dufranse eventually escapes from prison and crafts a cunning plan to both bring justice to a crooked warden and his staff, and to secure a nice retirement on a beach in Mexico somewhere. His escape is initially made possible by a few items he is able to secure via his friend and inmate Ellis Redding. Redding, or "Red" as he's called, provides a tiny rock hammer and a poster to Andy. During the day he uses the rock hammer to polish stones

from the prison yard into chess pieces that he

displays in his prison window. When no one is

looking he uses the tiny hammer to begin tunneling

his way through the cell walls. His escape route

was hidden the entire time in plain sight by the

poster of Rita Hayworth. As I watched the movie

and thought about his escape plan and how he

pulled it off, I thought about how many of us try to

escape from our own prisons. That is when a

lightbulb went off for me and reminded me how I

escaped from my own prison and cycle of poverty,

limited opportunity, and dead end soul sucking jobs.

There are three things that allowed Andy to escape

his prison cell and they revolve around his little rock

hammer. His rock hammer and how he utilized it hold the key for helping us understand how to create change in our own lives. In the next three chapters I'll give you the simple principles illustrated by Andy's escape and explain how you have everything you need to begin formulating and implementing your own escape to a better life. Stick with me to the end and you'll have everything you need to begin. Now if I were you, I would get on Amazon and rent or purchase The Shawshank Redemption. It's a great movie and if you watch it before you finish the next half of this book, I think it will help illustrate the key points I'm about to emphasize.

Chapter 6

Why Most People Swim Harder & Faster & Still Drown?

(Your Hammer)

So it wasn't until later in life that I realized how I could create success in my life. I unfortunately had to process through the best information I had at the time. So let me bring some clarity to a few philosophies that are in need of an upgrade.

Find A Good Job & Work Hard At It

The "find a good job and work hard at it", did allow

me to put food on the table and a roof over my

head but it wasn't the best food and the roof may

have had a few leaks. Worse, was the fact that in a

down economy I really felt the hit like the majority of

the country did.

Go To College & Get A Degree

Then there was the whole "Get a Bachelor's degree

and you'll be able to make good money. While

having a few years of college under my belt did

open up a few more opportunities it was far from

the financial freedom I hoped for. Even after getting my bachelor's degree I still had to start at a minimal salary, deal with office politics and boss's I didn't care much for, doing tasks that didn't elicit all of the talent, passion, and potential. The only difference is now I had student loan payments that were the same amount as my monthly mortgage. Two steps forward, three steps backwards. So what was the difference that made all the difference? Like most major shifts in life it all starts with your thinking.

A Mental Shift

My change came as the result of finding something I was interested in and which I saw had the potential to create the financial freedom and ability to travel that I wanted. However, just finding the vehicle didn't mean I was free of my paycheck to paycheck lifestyle as an employee and slave to the system I had so readily ascribed to. See I had to "do the work." So what follows in this chapter is a roadmap for "doing the work." In earlier chapters we talked about defining with clarity what you want to do, what you want to get, what you want to be, and what you want to contribute. Once you have that figured out you can then look at your activities, time and energy through the lens of the three things you can control. This will give you the ability to understand what you are doing and how you are doing it, so that you can make adjustments to achieve designing the life you want, at the pace you want, in the way you want. If you want to reach your goals faster, it can help you do that. If you want to ensure you aren't getting distracted by shiny object syndrome or the latest fads, it will do that too. It is a logical straight forward way of thinking that unfortunately I was never taught or modeled. So hopefully if you need this, it will save you years of frustration in trial and error. So let's get to it!

YOUR HAMMER

Why do some people work their ass off and never seem to get ahead financially? It's because their tool, method or vehicle is not up to the task. In The Shawshank Redemption, Andy was able to tunnel out of his prison cell using a tiny rock hammer. Now for the sake of this analogy, let's just imagine how much faster he could have gotten out with a sledge hammer, or a stick of dynamite. At the same time how long would it have taken him if all he had was his fingernails? Now it's time to slow down if you are speed reading and pay attention. This is extremely simple but you won't get it if you blow through this looking for an easy button.

Your ability to earn more money is directly related to the value you bring to the marketplace. Your ability to solve problems, your expertise is what will determine how much earning power you possess. Just like Andy had to settle for a tiny rock hammer, your earning power is like that hammer? Is it a tiny rock hammer, a fingernail, a sledgehammer, or a bulldozer? You might be running yourself ragged working multiple shifts, extra over-time, working harder than anyone else on the job and you're simply spent, exhausted and getting nowhere financially. Imagine if I give you magic goggles that give you the ability to see further and clearer than without them. Most people don't have these goggles. Because of this, they see the solution to their problem as, "I just need to find a better job that pays more." So they go from one crappy job to the next trying to get ahead and they have to wait for annual raises and promotions. Another downside is when the economy tanks it's like a reset button is hit and you risk having to start all over again, often settling for whatever work you can find. The worst part is, if this is where you are currently competing, then you are competing with the huge majority of people also looking for a job. There's less competition at the top. Finding a new job that pays a little more is not the solution to your problem.

Imagine I let you borrow my goggles and once you put them on you're no longer looking to "find a better job", but instead you start looking at yourself and how you can bring more value to the marketplace. Instead of looking to join a different ship, you start looking at how to make your own ship more capable. Instead of wishing you had a different prison cell (your circumstances), you start focusing on how to get out of that prison altogether. Upgrading your ability to bring value to the market place is like upgrading your hammer. The bigger your hammer, the more sophisticated and rare, the faster you can free yourself from your limiting circumstances. Upgrading your hammer will also multiply the effectiveness of the other two aspects we will discuss in the next two chapters. If you look at the three factors that can bring the most change in your life, this one will give you the most bang for your buck.

So specifically, how do you upgrade your hammer? Expertise. The market pays top dollar for expertise not general knowledge. If you were diagnosed with cancer, would you go to your local family physician, or would you seek out the top specialist & centers for beating cancer? Yeah me too, I'm seeing the specialist. In the same way you can improve your income not by being a jack of all trades, but by being an expert at one of them. Does that word expert intimidate you? It shouldn't. This shows the sad state our workforce is in, but did you know that if you read ten books on any single subject you would know more than 85% of the population about that one subject. Just by reading ten books focused on a single subject you are now more qualified than 85% of the population to give advice on that topic. Now imagine if you devoted your life to mastering that subject?

Be warned though, in this information age it's simply not enough to go to school. In fact that is a lot of people's problem. They graduated high school or college and just stopped learning. Stopped investing in themselves. You have unlimited potential. Every day, week, month and year brings you a new opportunity to expand your knowledge and improve your expertise and experience That means you have the opportunity to expand your potential over time. If your potential isn't limited then absolutely anything is achievable. Now you don't have all the time in the world, but you do have a lifetime. You simply have to find the intersection of what people want or need, and what you are passionate about and willing to spend your time and energy mastering. I have spent the last ten years learning and gaining experience in the arena of digital marketing and ecommerce. I still enjoy it and read books, listen to podcasts and purchase courses on it every month. Because I enjoy it I'm constantly learning and expanding my ability in this skill set. Something amazing happens when you gain a level of expertise in a certain skill. You no longer have to wait around for someone to hire you so you can earn an income. Instead, you now have the ability to create your own opportunity, your own business and create your own wealth.

The Process of Mastery

In this information age there's no shortage of ways to begin mastering your passion. There's podcasts, blogs, books, YouTube, Audible, forums, coaching &, college if necessary, and mentors. Whatever your budget allows, that's where you should begin. And don't just dabble. Become obsessed. You've got to be hungry and unstoppable in your pursuit of knowledge. When I started I watched YouTube videos, listened to audio books, and would buy print books from Goodwill. I've always told people I made more money from the knowledge I learned from buying books at Goodwill for a few bucks, than I did from my Bachelors degree which cost me tens of thousands of dollars more than my Goodwill education. If you're not motivated enough to learn to master something then you better get comfortable with the limitations of your current circumstances. Be warned though, the older you get the more responsibilities you'll have and the more money you need. So while you might have enough money now to keep your XBOX Live subscription and maintain your beer and pizza diet, that isn't likely to be the case. The fact that you're reading this book and you've made it this far tells me you're serious about transforming your life and making your dreams a reality.

When I chose digital marketing and ecommerce as my main skill to master I was also doing something really smart. In business you can leverage your time and skill to earn money. That's like the first level of earning power. Trading time for dollars. But the next level is leveraging other people's time, talent and energy to generate more revenue. That's the difference between being an employee vs an employer. The internet and online commerce has provided another level of earning power potential. With digital products or automated fulfilment you now have the potential to build a six or seven figure business and beyond and still have a fairly small operation. That means you can build a business that generates massive profits for less start up cost, less risk and less headaches than at any other time in history. So when you start thinking about how to upgrade your hammer, your earning power, you should at least do some research into how you can

leverage technology and automation.

Chapter 7

Laser or Squirt Gun
The Choice Is Yours

(Your Focus)

So the hammer was symbolic of your earning

power. Your expertise, your skill level. That is

probably the biggest lever you can utilize to move

the needle with your income. The second one you

should focus on is your focus. In The Shawshank

Redemption Andy tunnels to freedom using that tiny

rock hammer. Now can you imagine if every time he

chipped away at his prison walls he started in a

different spot, it would have taken him forever to

chip through that wall. He surely would have

missed his window of opportunity. This is the same

reason a lot of people fail. They fail to master

something simply because they are unfocused. You

know the type, maybe you are guilty of the same

thing. You start something with vigor and optimism

only to move on to the next thing when success

doesn't manifest overnight. We are all guilty of this

to some degree. With everything competing for our

attention, time, energy and resources we can easily

be spread so thin we become about as lethal as a

squirt gun. You know the example of light. Take

light and it's useful for lighting the room but that's

about it. But concentrate it and you can create a laser that's powerful enough to cut through steel. The same is true of our time and energy. The more focused we are with our efforts the greater our ability to create change becomes. When we combine the constant upgrading of our skills with focused effort and direction we discover the recipe for success. The real ability to create change. So let's dive into some practical ways to get focused.

Get Focused With Your Time

The older you get the more you realize we don't have all the time in the world. I was fifteen, I blinked and I was thirty, I sighed and now I'm in my 40's and 50 looms in the distance. It's absolutely crazy.

One of the most life changing beliefs for me was the moment I actually believed with conviction that I could do anything, I could learn anything and therefore I could become just about anything. Now that I'm in my forties I realize with the same amount of conviction and a bit of heartbreak, that while you could become anything, you do not have all the time in the world to accomplish it. It's just a fact that if you are going to master anything you need to narrow your focus. While you could become anything, you absolutely cannot master everything and you only have time to master one or at the most a few things. While it's said Prince could play some 27 instruments they are all musical instruments. So it's clear he set out to master music and musical creativity so even that was all in the same vein of skill.

Get Focused With Your Money

Once Andy had a clear plan of escape he sunk his pennies and smokes into bartering his way out. Sure he used what he had to purchase a rock, hammer, a poster, polishing cloth and such, but those were all tools used to make his escape. If you're serious about breaking out of the prison of a small earning power you're going to have to use the money you do have to invest in yourself. Don't blow your money on beer and hot wings. Man I love beer, hot wings and blue cheese dressing. If I had spent all my money on beer and wings I wouldn't have been able to make serious progress with my Goodwill education. You need to use everything you have to move you in the right direction. You need to focus all your resources and money on getting you closer to your goal of improving your earning power. That might mean saving your money for a book, a course, tuition, a mentor, a seminar, or it might me saving to make that first business investment in real estate or some other necessary purchase to get your business started.

While it means investing it also means cutting out the unnecessary expenses. It's time to make your operation as lean as possible to free up cash flow so you can invest it in yourself and in building your earning potential. If you're living below the poverty line but you have a house full of flat screens, a bumping stereo and a crap load of cable channels then you either need to invest in a more comfortable couch to set your ass down and get comfortable, or you need to cut out the crap and get serious about your goals. Take an inventory of your income and your expenses and realign and focus that money on things that will move you toward your goals.

Get Focused With Your Relationships

I love to party with my friends. There are times in your life when your bank account will be a direct reflection of how you are spending your time and who you spend it with. You have some friends that are perfectly happy living paycheck to paycheck and who constantly struggle to make ends meet. They are always telling you they don't have enough money to go on a quality trip or outing, but have no problem wasting day after day downing the beers in front of the television. Don't get me wrong. I love having friends over and catching the football games and watching the movies, but I'm able to enjoy them guilt free because I did the work to level up my skills and create automated income streams. You don't have a party at the bottom of the pit. Get yourself out first and then you'll have a reason and the resources to celebrate in style.

Make sure you are surrounded by goal oriented, disciplined people who inspire and challenge you to stay focused on your goals. If you're surrounded by people who complain about their problems and always place the blame on others and things they can't control rather than taking responsibility for where they are, then you need new friends. If you're friends are happy as a clam to spend hours talking about the lives of movie stars and sports athletes rather than taking strategy, goals, new things they are learning and so on, then you need new friends. You need friends who would rather binge learn than binge watch. Make sure they are people who show a genuine interest about your goals and who will push you and hold you accountable. When you get serious about your personal development it makes others around you uncomfortable. You'll quickly learn who are the motivated doers, the dreamers and talkers, and the *"leave me alone I'm perfectly happy the way I am."* Don't waste your time and energy trying to change them and don't be afraid to begin your journey alone. It's like going to the gym, just because nobody else wants to go doesn't change the fact that you need to get your ass in the gym and put the work in. When you set big goals and start moving towards them it will make those who are not like minded uncomfortable and some of them may express that in a negative way towards you. Don't take it personal, just give yourself space to grow so they don't pour cold water on the fire you're trying to get and keep burning.

Get Focused With Your Environment

You need to create some routine and routine spaces for learning. What will your learning habits look like? What your environment looks, feels and sounds like will impact your ability to progress. I do my best creative thinking in nature. That said, I can't always be out in nature so what do I do? I make sure my desk is next to a window. Something about natural light makes me feel better. If I'm in a dark room with no windows and no natural light I just can't focus at all. I don't know why but that's just me. Another thing I love is a big white board or chalk board. I love getting my thoughts and

business ideas out of my head and onto something

I can look at. I'm a big picture kind of guy and not a

details guy unless we are talking about data, but

that's another book for another time. Another thing

I'll do when I'm in work or learn mode is put on

some type of song with no lyrics or some other

song and just loop it. Not all songs do this for me.

Some distract me and get me focused on the music

instead of my work, but some I can literally loop for

hours while I work and it just helps keep my ADD

distracted while I crank out the work. You can get

more work done if you have your environment

dialed in to what works for you. You might have to

experiment with that to figure out what works for

you but it's worth it once you figure it out.

Optimize Your Life Around Your Focus

In order to create change in your life you have to

know what to focus on and how to get focused.

These seem like very simple and obvious thing but

this isn't always true. The pace of life and constant

distractions can keep us from ever realizing when

we are caught in the current and just going

wherever life takes us. If you are going to master

something you are going to have to master your

focus. Don't skip or downplay this important step

because if you get it wrong it could indefinitely

delay you from reaching your goal. Now we will get

to the last important aspect of this trifecta formula

for creating massive change in your life.

Chapter 8

This Is War

(Your Effort)

Once you learn how to work smarter, then you can masterfully apply the blunt force of all-out hard work. Imagine getting focused on a singular goal or objective. Maybe you've decided to finally get in top physical condition, or learn a new language, or get certification as an aviation mechanic. Perhaps you have your passion in sights and you're ready to start taking steps towards mastering that passion. If you put all your available focus, time, energy,

resources into mastering that one thing, how much

could your circumstances, opportunities and

income change in a few months or year? Are you

starting to see how practical yet profound this

simple strategy is? Once you are focused on a

clear and specific direction and you've optimized

your time and resources toward hitting that target,

you become unstoppable if you are persistent. So

what is the last factor? It's your effort. Just like

Andy Dufrane would spend each night carving out

his escape tunnel, you'll be working your plan for

escaping your income limitations. This is where that

effort and obsession take center stage. You can

escape that prison faster by upgrading your

hammer, focussing your work in one specific direction, and working your plan with speed, force and consistent repetition. A lot of people never get ahead simply because they don't put enough effort in to create momentum and change fast enough to keep themselves motivated. This is why you have to take massive action if you want to truly change your circumstances. There are plenty of books and audio books out there on how to stay motivated so I won't belabor that point except to say this, persistence is everything. So many people fail to start or quit shortly after they begin. Persistence is that magic differentiator between the lucky and the less fortunate. This is a muscle, a discipline that you must learn to exercise, grow and keep in shape because you'll need it to create any change, and you'll need it even more to maintain that change. If you don't know how to persistently work at mastering your skill during the times of struggle and during the times of wild success, you will certainly find yourself reminiscing about how successful you once were. That's certainly true about people who become and stay successful. Success isn't compiling the winning lottery numbers, it's not an event. Success isn't winning the Superbowl, it's implementing and sustaining the habits that get you to the Superbowl. In the same way creating higher levels of income and earning power in your life is not a singular event that happens, rather it is a journey of forming the right habits and philosophies

I really want to keep this chapter short and sweet so let me just drive the nail home. You have permission now to work your ass off so long as your work is focused on the right things. Your body and mind is the vehicle for creating this change so make sure you fuel it well, get your workout in. There is a reason most people who attain and maintain a high level of success have excellent nutrition and exercise habits. Having a healthy strong body that is well fueled will help you perform your best so don't neglect this aspect of upgrading your hammer. Now get to work and do it like you're a prisoner trying to escape prison. It's time to declare all-out war on the status quo and "good enough." Think about how much time, energy and money you've wasted doing the wrong things, headed in a hundred different directions, getting on the hamster wheel every day and never getting anywhere. Now imagine spending the rest of your life in this pointless cycle. Are you pissed yet? You can't get any of that time back, it's gone. What has it cost you? What have you missed out on? What will you miss out on if you don't make this shift, if you can't make yourself do the work? Is it worth it? Don't waste anymore time. Don't let the regrets stack up on you. Get busy doing the work and keep at it! You'll be so glad you did.

Chapter 9

Conclusion

I learned how to work hard when I was young. As a young married man I worked hard at my job working in a warehouse. It was in that warehouse one hot summer in Texas that I decided I would rather work smarter than harder. That way of thinking continued to evolve until I arrived at the place where I began to work hard on myself. As Jim Rohn says, "If you work hard at your job you can make a living, but if you work hard on yourself you can make a fortune." Reflecting on my life, and how

I made the leap from few income prospects and an anemic bank account, to creating my own income opportunities and earning multiple six figures annually, I whittle it down to the previously mentioned overlapping principles. 1.) An all out effort and disciplined focus on mastering a singular high value skill that you love and can commit to mastering. 2.) A laser focus in and executing with that skill. 3.) An all out sacrificial effort and the speed, frequency and consistency of executing with that skill. That understanding alone can help you break free if you find yourself trapped in a dead end rut. While there are a ton of self-help, personal development, and business books available, your approach to learning and the application of that knowledge can make or break you. It's not about how wide and fast you go, but about how consistently and quickly, you can go deep in a particular subject or skill.

A few more things to consider. Part of what made our success curve so great was catching the front end of a new trend. Anytime you can be a part of something while it is in it's early and explosive growth stage, that will only amplify your success. When we started our first business we were one of the first major players to enter and we did have an advantage. Our marketing and automation was more comprehensive and strategic while being much leaner than our competitors. This helped solidify our position as one of the market leaders and made it more difficult for other new competitors to enter in and survive. As your market category ages and more options come available that same first to marketing leverage helps you compete because you have way more brand authority, trust, customer reviews, and data to leverage to help give your business an advantage.

The other advantage we had from a scalable income standpoint was that most of the time all the work required was manageable between just myself and my wife. That kept us extremely lean. While others were going out of business and laying off employees, we were still making profits and growing the business. We were able to spend more on acquiring a customer because it cost us less to create and deliver our products and there was more profit due to that low overhead. We were able to stay lean because of automation. In this digital age people are not just consumers of physical products or info that is delivered in a physical medium, but it is increasingly becoming a world of digital transactions and delivery of that information.

Think about this. What kind of infrastructure would I have to have to teach 10 different one hour courses in every state and country around the world? You'd have to have instructors, materials, a registration process, administrators, facilities and all the red tape involved in setting up something like that in each city, state, country, language etc. But could I curate or create ten one hour courses delivered via video and make that available to the entire world all by myself? Yes indeed you can! The first would take months if not years to set up, and even longer to get feedback on if it's working, profitable or even sustainable. Leveraging digital automation you could record your course material with your iPhone and have them uploaded to the web in one day. You could create the site to manage delivery of those courses the next day and be making sales by day two or three. Not to mention with tools like Google Analytics and digital advertising you could have feedback instantly. This would allow you to start optimizing your offers for profit from the day you go live. Are you the type of person that has a lot of creative ideas for a business. If they are digital, you can test them all and determine if they are viable so you can narrow your focus to your best options based on real data and feedback.

It's truly a unique and exciting time to be an entrepreneur. I really hope the ideas I've shared in this book can help you start to gain momentum in creating a better life for yourself. Remember one thing I know for sure. If you don't believe it's possible for you then, nothing I say or do can make it come true for you. However, once you determine that it's possible for yourself, you'll already possess the seeds required for great success. Then you just have to persist in doing the work. I wish you all the best!